Cocktail Recipes

Sensational & Easy Cocktail Recipes for Every Season

(Includes more than 60 delicious recipes!)

Bowe Packer

TABLE OF CONTENTS

Publishers Notes

Disclaimer

This publication is intended to provide helpful and informative material on cocktail recipes. It is not intended to be a full bartenders guide.

With that said, please understand that the author made every attempt to provide sound information at a reasonable price. There are things you will encounter on this journey of making good cocktails that the author did not. That is just the way life works.

The author and publisher specifically disclaim all responsibility for any liability, loss or risk, personal or otherwise, which is incurred as a consequence, directly or indirectly, from the use or application of any contents of this book.

Any and all product names referenced within this book are the trademarks of their respective owners. None of these owners have sponsored, authorized, endorsed, or approved this book.

Paperback Edition 2013

Manufactured in the United States of America

DEDICATION

I dedicate this book to all those people out there who remind us of the things we have forgotten about ourselves.

And this holds especially true of my beautiful and amazing wife, Alma. She is the one woman who has the most amazing talent to let me grow and love the things about myself that I have not fully accepted.

I cherish the love she has for me when I may not know how to love myself.

May we all have this kind of beautiful soul in our life.

Sent from LOVE,

Sunshine In My Soul

How To Make the Most of This Book

If you are the type of person that likes having parties and having people over for drinks then this is definitely the book for you. You're going to want to know all different types of drinks and different ways to enjoy a great cocktail party. Well this book is going to help you figure those things out. You'll learn about the many different kinds of cocktails available and you'll also learn how to make them. We have a lot of recipes in later chapters of this book so you can enjoy a great time with your friends (both drinkers and non-drinkers alike.

This book also has a section on how to throw a great party the very first time and how to pair up some great snacks with the cocktails that you choose. There's a lot you need to know about cocktail parties from the proper mixes to the best cocktails to serve all the way to which glasses you should serve each drink in. Each chapter in this book is geared towards helping you have an amazing party and a highly accurate one as well. It's going to be a fun and interesting time for you to learn brand new recipes and have a great time with your friends all at the same time.

PART I:- GETTING STARTED

What you may not realize is that cocktails are actually a primary ingredient in a lot of social gatherings and even professional occasions. People like to have a drink or two because it helps them to relax. So do you want to join the group of people who love making new cocktails and having great, fun drinks with your friends all the time? Well chances are that you probably do because having fun with your friends is the primary reason that you get together with them at all isn't it? If you weren't having fun then you might as well just stay home.

As you read through this book you're going to learn about some great new drinks to make and some ways to really have a good time. Personally I'm no bartender but I'm pretty sure that you'll find recipes that you really will enjoy, even if you've never heard of them before. Don't be afraid to give new things a chance. After all, you're planning to be a cocktail partier for the first time right?

Chapter 1- Your First Party

Okay so now you've set up your first party but you're not sure what to do next. Maybe you're a little worried about what's going to happen or what you're going to do. Well not to worry because we are here to help you out with those questions. That's because absolutely anyone can have a cocktail party and you can all have a great cocktail party that people will talk about for a long time to come. It's just a matter of knowing a few simple things.

The first thing you need to figure out (after you've created your guest list anyway) is what drinks you're going to be making. Now the idea of serving your guests absolutely any drink they may want probably sounds exciting and fun. It makes you the master of everything because you can mix up absolutely any kind of drink that you want. It's also great for all of your friends because they get to drink whatever their favourite beverage is. So that sounds great right? Well the truth of the matter is that it's not as great as it sounds.

When you offer a larger range of drinks to your guests not only do you have to spend more time learning how to make all those beverages but you'll also have to stay behind the bar and make all the drinks continuously. You're also going to have a harder time keeping up with drink orders if you have a lot of different choices. So remember that you're going to want to start out slowly and take it a little easier. You'll want to have only a few options for any cocktail party where there are less than 20 people possibly even parties with thirty people. This is because you want to be able to perfect your drink choices and you also don't want to make people wait too long to get the beverage of their choice.

It's possible that you can even prepare drinks before your party so all you have to do is pour them out or simply hand the party goer a glass with a pre-mixed drink already in it. These can be very simple and they can definitely help you if you're going to be pressed for time once all of those guests start arriving. But they're not going to be quite as good as the drinks that you whip up right on the spot. You'll want to remember that at least one or two of your drinks should be freshly mixed each time they are requested so you don't just have a bunch of pitchers you're serving out of.

A blender is going to be your best friend for mixing up these drinks and for preparing some others. You'll want it because you'll need crushed ice for a lot of your recipes and it's not going to be easy crushing up ice without one. You don't have to spend a lot of money you just need to make sure the blender you choose is capable of crushing up ice because not all blenders are and then you'd be left with something that really won't help you in the long run. This makes your drinks smooth and keeps your guests coming back for more.

CHAPTER 2- THE IMPORTANCE OF FRESH ICE

Do you know how ice really works? Well it keeps your drinks and things cold of course but what happens when it sits too long? If you leave ice out for too long (even in a freezer) it begins to absorb smells and tastes. This means when you put that ice into your cocktail (and you're going to use a lot of ice in a cocktail) then you're going to be giving your guest a little bit of the flavour of your frozen beef and leftovers. Those or things you don't want them to taste in your cocktails because they're not all that appetizing.

You need to make sure the ice you are using is fresh. That means you're going to need to purchase it on the day of the party or you're going to want to make it up in your home freezer no more than one day before the event. This helps to ensure that your ice tastes like nothing but water so it doesn't conflict with the excellent flavour of your cocktails. You want your guests to keep coming back because of the excellent flavour and not to ask what that strange taste is as the ice begins to melt.

Now when you're making cocktails there are a few different kinds of ice that you're going to want to know about. Each one can be a good choice for your party but each one is also going to have a little bit different 'skill' for your party. You're going to want to consider all of your options.

1. Cracked Ice-this is probably one of the most common and most well-known types of ice to use for cocktail parties. It tends to melt faster than regular ice as you might imagine because air is able to get into the cracks must faster. On the other hand this can be easier to crush with a blender because the cracks help the blender gain purchase and keep you from breaking or dulling the sharp edges of your blender. Cracked ice can take up to 1 cup in order to make one cocktail.

2. Shaved Ice-If you're making snow cones with liquor in them you'll probably want shaved ice. This is because the consistency is going to be much more authentic and taste much better if you use the right type of ice. You can use cracked or regular cubes for this type of 'drink' but you'll be better off choosing shaved.

3. Japanese Ice Balls- Made popular in the bars of Japan these balls are actually very good at not melting. In Japan they tend to make these balls by hand but you don't have to do that. You can actually purchase moulds which will help you to create a perfectly round ball that will help keep your guests drinks cold without causing the normal problems of watering them down within only minutes of making them in the first place.

CHAPTER 3- SNACKING IS IMPORTANT

So you're looking to have a cocktail party and you've got the drinks all figured out. You know how to make them perfectly and you know who you're inviting but what are you feeding these people? You don't need to plan a full five-course (or even three-course) meal. But you are going to need to have some good snacks. You don't want all those people drinking on an empty stomach after all.

So what should you serve to help your guests stay sober and still have a good time? Well believe it or not you can serve dairy products to your guests. This helps to limit the amount of alcohol that is absorbed into their system and also helps keep them from getting hungry and leaving in search of food. Of course dairy products can sometimes be complicated when it comes to snacks. Serving cheese is the traditional snack in European countries however this doesn't always work with Americans. Instead, find some other cheese based snack to serve.

Another important thing to have at your party is water. You don't want your guests getting thirsty and guzzling a lot of alcohol. If you serve water they're more likely to slow down their drinking which means you get to have fun with your friends for a longer period of time without having to deal with a lot of drunks.

CHAPTER 4- CAN YOU SHAKE IT

No we're not talking about on the dance floor. We're talking about whether you know how to make up a cocktail properly. It's all about that special shake that bartenders have perfected. You know those silver shakers that nearly every bar around the country has. The bartender puts the drinks in there and shakes it up. That means you need to make sure that you have a shaker of your own and that you understand how to make it.

There are a few different types of shakers however you'll really only need to know about a couple. The French shaker has two pieces without a strainer which you will likely want because it helps to get the crushed ice pieces out (the ones that are too big anyway). A Boston shaker or Cobbler shaker on the other hand will be perfect for your needs without any extra pieces. Whichever type you choose to buy you'll be off to a great start and you'll be ready to go once you learn that shake.

Shaking a drink should be done with your moving your wrist up and down. This shakes the drink slightly but not too much. It should also take only about twenty seconds. One way to tell easily if the drink is mixed properly is that there will be slight condensation on the surface of your shaker. That's what happens when the chilled ice cools the rest of the drink. It means you're ready to serve. So that's when you're going to take off the cap and pour your drink into a glass. Make sure there are only three ice cubes in each glass so you don't dilute the drink with water.

CHAPTER 5- THE PROPER GLASS FOR EACH DRINK

There are a lot of different kinds of bar glasses that you're going to want to check out before you have your party. Of course you don't need to purchase absolutely every kind of bar glass there is unless you're planning to actually open a bar. But you are going to want to look into them and see which glasses you need for your cocktail party. These are some of the most popular types of drink glasses and what you can serve in them.

1. Champagne Glass-These glasses have very long stems and only hold small amounts of liquid. They are commonly used for weddings and formal occasions (at least in their flute form) but there are goblets and saucer glasses as well in this form. The flutes are extremely slim and tall while goblets have a round base (and are slightly bigger). Saucers on the other hand are very large around with a round base.

2. Martini Glass-A martini glass is the one you've probably used most if you go to bars or restaurants. These are quite popular and have long stems like champagne glasses. Unlike champagne glasses

however they have a wider rim and are capable of being downed in one long drink. They also hold about four ounces rather than two like most champagne glasses.

3. Liqueur Glass-These are slightly smaller glasses as they have very thick bases and a narrow appearance. They hold only about three ounces and are generally used for appetizer cocktails.

4. Tall Cocktail Glass-These are similar to liqueur glasses however they tend to be much taller. If you are using a drink that calls for juice as a main ingredient you could use one of these taller glasses which hold approximately ten ounces of liquid instead of the three ounces of liqueur glasses.

5. Rock Glass-These are typically used for pure forms of alcohol. They are short and round with heavy bottoms. They hold pure drinks like gin or rum that isn't mixed rather than regular cocktails and hold approximately six ounces.

6. Collin's Glass-This is a straight glass that is tall. They are very simple and actually if you have a drink glass

which holds approximately eight ounces then you probably don't even need this type of drink glass.

Chapter 6- The Arsenal

So you've got everything else figured out and now you need the equipment to get started. There are actually only a few things you're going to need but they are all extremely important so make sure you don't forget anything. It's not going to cost much to invest in these things and you can find them just about anywhere you normally shop.

1. Double Jigger-This is a type of measuring device that helps you to get exact measures of the ingredients you're adding to your cocktails. It's important to know the measurements exactly and get them right so your drinks all taste the same and they all taste good. You don't want to mix up your measures and have a drink come out all wrong.

2. Boston Shaker-These are very important and have a built in strainer as well as a metal cap. You want to make sure you get a stainless steel shaker rather than a plastic one because you'll be able to see the condensation on the outside which tells you that it's time to stop shaking and serve.

3. Mixing Glasses-Some drinks need to be mixed but not in their glasses. These mixing glasses are approximately ten ounces and have a heavy base so you don't have to worry about them tipping. They also have a small spout so that the drink can be easily poured into a proper glass once it's been mixed.

4. Cocktail Strainer-Strainers are very important so that you can keep extra ice from getting into your glasses. You definitely don't want too much because it can cause the drink to become diluted and some drinks you really don't want excess ice in at all. In most cases you won't need a hand strainer if you've already gotten a Boston Shaker but for drinks that don't need to be shaken you'll have a better chance with one of these.

5. Blender-Remember that you need to have some way of crushing ice. Ice can cause damage to a normal blender sometimes so make sure you are ready for the event that your blades may become dull or you may end up with dings and scratches in your blender. All you need to do is blend the ice and then pour it into your Boston shaker.

Another option for this is an ice crusher which is a manual method of breaking ice into smaller pieces however this can become tiring after some time because you need to crush all of the ice entirely by hand which slows you down as well.

6. Long Spoon-You're going to need a way to mix your drinks that need to be swirled without being shaken. So make sure you understand the length of your glasses so you can get a good size spoon that will help you to reduce spilling.

CHAPTER 7- THE SPIRIT OF THE SEASON

There's another step we need to go through before we get into the recipes and that's the alcohol itself. So we're going to give you a brief overview of the typically used liqueurs in these types of cocktails and how you should be using them. If you don't understand your alcohol after all then it becomes much more difficult to actually make a mixed drink and you definitely won't be able to create your own mixed drinks unless you understand more.

Vodka- This is a very pure spirit with nearly no taste. This means you can use it in pretty much anything you want and it will go together. Whether you like sweet, sour or spicy, vodka can be your best friend. It's made by fermenting some native grains and then distilled to remove nearly every aspect but the alcohol.

Bourbon-Now this is a type of alcohol that is aged to produce a smoky flavor. It's fermented with a lot of different grains and then stored in oak barrels for several years before it's ever brought out and served. It actually takes at least two years to get bourbon to a stage where it can be used and then it's best when mixed with sour or bitter ingredients.

Rum-Made from fermented juice from sugar cane rum also includes a little caramel. This is a very popular drink with many crowds.

Cachaca-This one you may not have heard of (unless you're a drink connoisseur) but it is a very popular drink. It's made from fermented sugar cane (not the juice used in rum) and it's never mixed with anything before you put it in a drink. It can be used straight or it can be mixed with tropical drinks though you can also use rum in many of the same drinks.

Tequila-This is a very strong drink known to come from Mexico. It has a pretty powerful taste and it's made from fermented agave which is a plant native to Mexico. It needs to be stored in wood barrels at least four years before it can be drunk or sold. If you haven't drunk tequila before then you should understand the process of taking a drink straight, place a little salt in the palm of your hand and lick it off then drink the shot of tequila and follow it up with a bite of a lime.

Tequila can be found in clear or tinted forms. Clear tequila doesn't have an aging process to it but it does still have a strong flavor. Golden or tinted tequila on the other hand has a deeper color and will be even stronger from the fermenting and aging process. This is the more popular form of the drink.

Gin-Another very popular alcoholic drink is gin. There are plenty of ways that you can use this beverage and there's no doubt you'll be using at least one of them. It's made from fermentation of berries rather than grains and is then mixed with different types of spices. Most of the time gin will be drunk straight with a little ice but you can mix it will tonic water or sour/bitter ingredients.

Cognac-came from France and needs to be aged in oak bottles for some time before drinking. It works best when mixed with citrus or even chocolates.

Campari-This type of liqueur is used as an appetizer cocktail and has approximately 25% alcohol content. Usually you will mix this with a couple fresh fruit juices, tonic water or club soda though it can be mixed with regular types of champagne as well.

Vermouth-This is created using spices and herbs and has a similar taste to gin.

Orange Spirits-These have up to 40% alcohol content and can be mixed with vodka, rum, dry gin or citrus juices.

Cream Liqueur-Make sure you use real fruit juices with these types of liqueur and that you use corresponding juices with the juice already in the drink.

Coconut Spirits-This is becoming a more common and popular drink and it can actually be mixed with a lot of different flavors. For the most part however this is a tropical beverage so mix it appropriately.

CHAPTER 8- DRINK INGREDIENTS

Remember of course that there are other ingredients in drinks rather than just the ones that we've mentioned above. Outside of liqueur you're going to want to add in some good ingredients and flavors as well so you can make something that tastes good and not just like straight alcohol.

Flavor-You want to make sure your drink has a good flavor and that's not always the strong taste of alcohol. The best method for flavoring alcohol however is to make sure you use fresh ingredients such as strawberries, lemons, herbs or peppers. This way you get the full flavor and a natural one as well.

If you want to try something particular then experiment with gin or vodka. You'll want to add the fresh ingredients and then put the sealed bottle in a dark area for at least one month. The flavor will seep into the alcohol and the longer you leave it the longer that flavor will continue to be absorbed.

Puree-A fruit puree is important if your drink recipe calls for it. You need to make sure that you're using any puree that your recipe asks for because it will counteract any problems there might be with the alcohol such as negative characteristics. Make sure you use fresh fruit and create your own puree rather than using jars or pre-made puree.

Making the puree just requires 1 tbsp. of sugar syrup and however much of the fruit that your recipe asks for. Remember to use only 1 tbsp. for the entire amount requested in the puree recipe unless that recipe tells you something different. You don't want to add too much sugar or your drink is definitely not going to turn out properly.

Sugar Syrup-You're going to need a type of sweetener in just about every recipe that you use so make sure you have sugar syrup on hand. There are some methods other than this such as citrus twists or candied ginger but you'll probably be safe with sugar syrup in your bar. If you are interested you can actually make your own sugar syrup by mixing two hundred grams of pure white table sugar with two hundred fifty milliliters of clean mineral water.

All you need to do is mix them in a saucepan until they come to a boil. You'll want the stove on medium heat and use a stainless steel stirrer to break down the sugar crystals better. You'll end up with a melted, smooth syrup which you'll want to cool in the pot until it's cooled enough to transfer to a glass jar. You can then refrigerate the jar or start using it right away.

Now you can use demerara sugar in place of table sugar which provides a slightly different flavor. It is sweet with a strong flavor in fact and a higher content of molasses. Remember however that because demerara sugar has a flavor (distinctly molasses flavored) it can mix badly with certain cocktail recipes. It can also cause a slight tint to your drinks because it's darker in color than traditional table sugar.

Sugar syrup will spoil over time (in fact approximately one month after it's made you will have to make new sugar syrup). If you mix in one tablespoon of pure vodka into the mixture however it will last for approximately three months rather than one. Make sure you use one tablespoon per batch (and no more) to get the best results.

Flavored Syrup- A flavored syrup will help to add some flavor but not alcoholic content to your drinks. They do have some alcohol in them so be careful if you're making drinks for a younger group as well as an adult one but they won't add enough that most will be able to notice.

CHAPTER 9- THINGS YOU WILL WANT TO REMEMBER

If you're planning on making drinks for friends for the first time you're going to want to know these five simple tips.

1. The quality of your alcohol is going to affect the flavor of your drinks. That is to say if you buy a $10 bottle of rum you're going to get the flavor of a $10 bottle of rum whereas the flavor of a $50 bottle of rum is likely going to be more what you're after. Of course you probably don't have the money to go out and buy a lot of $50 bottles of liqueur for a party and your first attempt at cocktails. Luckily you don't have to.

    What you need to do is make sure that you are weighing out and finding a balance between the flavor of your drinks and the amount of money you have available to spend. Look for something that will give you a reasonable amount of good for the money that you're spending on it. You want to get at least middle of the road alcohol for your trouble.

2. Make sure your glasses are the temperature of the drink you're serving. That means you may want to make sure that your drink glasses are stored at the right temperature. You may want to put some of them in the fridge or freezer to keep them cold while others you may want to keep warm depending on the type of drink that you are making.

3. Not all of your drinks are going to require garnishes even though you can add a garnish to any or all drinks. Make sure if you do however you are not influencing the flavor of the drink in a bad way with your garnish of choice. If there's supposed to be a specific garnish on a drink however (such as olives with a martini) make sure you use the correct one.

4. Fresh fruit is much better than canned fruits and you will definitely be able to taste the difference. There's a stronger flavor and there's also less chemicals and additives that you really don't want in your drinks anyway. So try (as much as possible) to use fresh fruit rather than opting in for canned or frozen fruits.

5. Make sure everything that goes into your drink is properly measured. If you want to experiment with quantities you want to make sure that you're doing it

for yourself and not when you're in the middle of a cocktail party. For the time being, stick to the recipe exactly as it reads.

CHAPTER 10- A PROPER GARNISH

You want to make sure that you have a good garnish on each of your drinks but remember that you don't need to spend a lot of time or effort to have a good garnish for your drink. It's just important to understand the basics and to do what needs to be done for specialty drinks. Just remember these key traits for the beginning and you can experiment later.

Cocktail Umbrellas-These paper umbrellas are extremely inexpensive and can be used in just about any drink because they won't change the flavor. They just add a little tropical feel and who doesn't love that?

Sweetened & Salted Rims-If you want a rim with salt or sugar you'll need fruit syrup or liqueur (cream liqueur) that you can pour onto a clean plate. Then you tip the glass upside down on the plate and carefully pick it up to get some of the syrup to stick to the glass. Next you put sugar or salt on a second plate and dip the rim of the glass in that. When you pick up the glass you'll have a nice rim of sugar or salt.

Fruit Garnish-Make sure these match your cocktail very well since you're going to end up with some juices in the drink.

You want to cut the fruit into chunks and put them on toothpicks or small skewers. Then put them on top of the glass.

Citrus Twist-These are just the peelings of a fruit like lemon or lime. All you do is take a peeler and peel the fruit in a spiral. Cut the spiral in half and hang it on the edge of the glass.

Sweet Swirls-if you want something sweet you'll want to add in fruit syrup or cream liqueur with a spoon. Apply it to the sides of the glass and then let it move its own way down to the bottom of the drink.

Fruit Cubes-The last of the very simple options we have is to use fruit juice frozen into ice cubes. These give you flavored and colorful treats for your drinks.

CHAPTER 11- MOCKTAILS FOR ALL

Sometimes you'll have guests who will ask for cocktails without any alcohol. No need to fret! Below are some easy cocktail recipes that don't require alcoholic spirits. Serve one or two at your cocktail party, and you'll have no problem with non-drinkers.

Taste of the Caribbean

1. You'll need one fourth cup of the following: fresh orange juice, fresh pineapple juice, and some sweet peach nectar. Combine these juices first in the shaker.

2. Add four teaspoons of plain cherry juice to the existing mix, and a small amount of fresh lime juice (one eighth cup should do). Once the citrus flavors have combined, add four tsp. of cream of coconut.

3. For the finishing step, add half a teaspoon of grenadine. Shake the final mix for just twenty seconds before straining. Pour the cocktail over four plain or garnished ice cubes.

The Dragon's Lair

1. For this cocktail, you'll need one third cup of any fruit-flavored tea (you need red tea for this one), one fourth cup of blood-orange nectar, and four tsp. of freshly squeezed lime juice. Combine these ingredients in a tall mixing glass.

2. Add an additional two tsp. of cream of coconut and the same amount of light almond syrup. With a long handled mixing spoon, stir the resulting mix well until the creation is evenly blended.

3. Serve the Dragon's Lair in a Collin's glass or a tall, plain glass. Garnish with fruit or a citrus twist.

Fruity Surprise

1. For this cocktail, you'll need a good, old-fashioned blender. You'll need one fourth cup of cantaloupe, one fourth cup of papaya, one fourth cup of mango, and one fourth cup of fresh orange juice.

2. After mixing the first batch of ingredients, add one fourth cup of nectar of the passion fruit and just four tsp. of lemon juice. As a finishing touch, add four tsp. of light almond syrup to the concoction. Add the equivalent of three ice cubes worth of crushed ice.

3. Blend the creation for a few seconds and pour into a tall glass.

Ginger Delight

1. For this recipe, you'll need just one piece of ginger that has been preserved in sugar syrup. Take one piece from the jar and dice finely. Add this to the glass.

2. Next, add one tsp. of fresh juice from a pear (use a juicer). Add the same amount of grape juice. (Use *white grape juice* for this recipe.)

Pour just enough ginger ale in the glass to fill it past the half-full mark. Add three to four ice cubes, stir a little, and serve.

PART II:- THE COCKTAILS

This section of the book contains top-notch cocktail recipes from bars from around the country, and around the world. Some of these cocktails are invigorating, some are stimulating, and others are better mixed when you want a soothing, relaxing night. Experiment with the ones you like and remember the ones you think your guests will love. Good luck!

PINEAPPLE RUM MIX

For the Pineapple Rum Mix, you will need the entire shell of a large pineapple, cut into two. The top portion of the pineapple should be intact and cleanly cut from the other half.

Simply remove the contents of the pineapple, freeze the shell, and cut a small hole on top so that a straw can be inserted. Place the top half of the pineapple and insert a straw when the cocktail is ready. The walls of the pineapple shell should be no thinner than twelve millimeters. The flesh of the fruit should be kept, as a portion of this will be used in the actual cocktail.

Ingredients:

- 1 pineapple (shell & flesh)
- 132 milliliters of golden rum
- 33 ml fresh lime juice
- 22 ml sugar syrup (you can buy commercial sugar syrup or you can create your own at home by combining water and sugar. The ratio should be two to one).

Steps:

- Slice off the hard part of the pineapple flesh. Place the soft flesh in the blender and add the equivalent of twelve ounces of ice to the mix. The ice should be crushed first, to facilitate the blending of the pineapple flesh.

- Add the remaining ingredients (golden rum, lime juice, sugar syrup) and blend for a few seconds.

- Pour into the pineapple shell that you have prepared beforehand.

CREAMY STRIPED SHOT

To make the Creamy Striped Shot, you will need to chill all the ingredients first -- and don't forget to chill the glass as well. After chilling everything for some minutes, pour the following ingredients *in order* to create the striped effect. The varying colors of the spirits will create the striped effect. Use a plain shot glass for this one.

Ingredients:

- 22 ml amaretto
- 22 ml cream liqueur
- 22 ml cognac

LIME-CACHACA MIX

The Lime-Cachaca Mix is best served in a tall serving glass like a Collin's glass. Serve with a pineapple wedge as well, if you can. Keep the hard shell of the pineapple on, as it helps accentuate the green hue of this refreshing drink. Simply mix the ingredients listed below and shake in a Boston shaker. Strain and serve over a few cubes of ice.

Ingredients:

- 110 ml of cachaca
- 132 ml of fresh pineapple juice
- 22 ml of sugar syrup
- 22 ml of lemon juice

MINTY ABSINTHE

The Minty Absinthe is best served in a long-stemmed martini glass, with a fresh mint leaf garnish placed directly into the drink. Simply shake the ingredients to create the drink.

Ingredients:

- 44 ml of absinthe (66% proof)
- 44 ml of water
- 11 ml of sugary syrup

ORANGE VERMONT

Serve the Orange Vermont in a chilled martini glass and garnish with a citrus twist -- orange is ideal. Shake the ingredients and pour over ice.

Ingredients:

- 88 ml dry gin
- 44 ml dry vermouth
- 44 ml fresh orange juice
- 2.7 ml of Angostura Bitters flavoring

CARAMEL ABSINTHE

Serve the Caramel Absinthe in a chilled martini glass. This cocktail must be served with a citrus twist, preferably lemon. Use a Boston shaker to mix this drink. Another variant of this recipe requires crushed ice *in* the martini glass prior to pouring the mixed cocktail.

Ingredients:

- 44 ml of absinthe (68% proof)
- 11 ml of almond syrup
- 11 ml of Anisette liqueur
- .9 ml of Angostura bitters flavoring
- 33 ml of water

ABSINTHE WITH SUGAR DRIP

For this recipe, you'll need an absinthe spoon and a regular sugar cube. After preparing the cocktail, place the sugar cube on top of the absinthe spoon.

Pour a small amount of water over the sugar cube so that the sugar is slowly dissolved. The resulting sweet solution will slowly drip into the absinthe cocktail. Add a few ice cubes to the finished cocktail before serving. Use a Boston shaker to create this cocktail.

Ingredients:

- 88 ml of water
- 1 cube of sugar
- 66 ml of absinthe (68% proof)

SWEET ABSINTHE & ANISETTE MIX

This is a fairly regular cocktail that requires only shaking in a Boston shaker and a regular citrus twist. (Use lemon. If lemon isn't available, use lime). Chill a martini glass and pour the mix into the glass with a few ice cubes.

Ingredients:

- 44 ml of absinthe (68% proof)
- 22 ml of anisette liqueur
- 11 ml of maraschino liqueur
- 66 ml of water

ORANGE & AROMATIC ABSINTHE

This recipe is for absinthe lovers who prefer a cornucopia of flavors when enjoying their beloved spirit. Shake the ingredients in a Boston shaker and serve in a chilled, long-stemmed martini glass.

Ingredients:

- 44 ml of absinthe (68% proof)
- 33 ml of dry gin
- 11 ml of anisette liqueur
- .9 ml of orange bitters
- .18 ml of Angostura bitters flavoring
- 66 ml of water

MINTY FRAPPE

Serve Minty Frappe in a rock glass or heavy-bottomed old-fashioned glass. After combining the ingredients in a Boston shaker, shake for twenty seconds and pour into the glass. The glass must have crushed ice prior to the pouring.

With a long-handled mixing spoon, mix the cocktail for a few seconds and garnish with a fresh sprig of mint on top of the crushed ice. Do all of this quickly enough, and the crushed ice will simply float to the top of the cocktail, which adds to the overall experience of drinking the Minty Frappe.

Ingredients:

- 66 ml of absinthe (68% proof)
- 22 ml of anisette liqueur
- 66 ml of water
- 11 ml of sugar syrup

SWISS ABSINTHE

Again, this absinthe creation should be served in a rock glass. Shake the ingredients in a shaker, strain, and serve over ice cubes. Some people like adding egg whites to the Swiss Absinthe. It's entirely up to you. It can be done, but it's not completely essential to the cocktail.

Ingredients:

- 66 ml of absinthe (68% proof)
- 22 ml of almond-flavored syrup
- 22 ml of heavy cream
- 22 ml of milk

CREAMY ABSINTHE

Serve Creamy Absinthe in a shot glass with a long-stemmed handle. Ingredients of the Creamy Absinthe cocktail are to be layered one after the other in a glass that has been chilled in the freezer for a minute or two.

Ingredients:

- 33 ml of Pisang Ambon liqueur
- 33 ml of cream liqueur
- 22 ml of absinthe (68% proof)

CHERRY ABSINTHE

Serve the Cherry Absinthe in a long-stemmed martini glass. Shake in a Boston shaker, strain, and pour into a chilled martini glass. Garnish the cocktail with a single Maraschino cherry. Egg whites can be added -- this is optional and is entirely up to you.

Ingredients:

- 88 ml of dry gin
- 22 ml of Grenadine syrup
- 22 ml of double cream
- 22 ml of fresh milk

CRANBERRY-VODKA DELIGHT

The Cranberry-Vodka Delight is best served in a tall, chilled flute champagne glass. First, combine the vodka and the cranberry juice in a Boston shaker. Strain the resulting mix and pour into the glass. Pour the champagne last, and garnish with a single strawberry.

Ingredients:

- 44 ml of vodka
- 88 ml of cranberry juice
- 22 ml of champagne

FANCY DAIQUIRI

Serve the Fancy Daiquiri in a long-stemmed martini glass. After shaking in a Boston shaker, pour the resulting cocktail into the martini glass and lightly dust the surface with cocoa powder. Add just enough floating powder to the cocktail to create the perfect balance of color.

Ingredients:

- 88 ml of rum
- 22 ml of white cream of chocolate
- 22 ml of lime juice
- 11 ml of sugar syrup

PINEAPPLE-RUM SOOTHER

Serve the Pineapple-Rum Soother in a tall, pre-chilled glass, and garnish the finished cocktail with pineapple wedge. All ingredients must be shaken before serving.

Ingredients:

- 44 ml of tequila
- 44 ml of golden rum
- 44 ml of grapefruit juice
- 110 ml of pineapple juice
- 22 ml of sugar syrup

RASPBERRY RUM MIX

Serve the Raspberry Rum Mix in a tall cocktail glass or Collin's glass. After shaking, the finished cocktail should be garnished with a single slice of apple.

Ingredients:

- 88 ml of vodka
- 11 ml of black raspberry-flavored liqueur
- 11 ml of peach schnapps liqueur
- 44 ml of fresh apple juice
- 22 ml of fresh lemon juice

LIGHT DAIQUIRI

Serve the Light Daiquiri in a chilled martini glass. Shake all ingredients in a Boston shaker and strain. Pour into a chilled glass – no ice cubes needed for this cocktail!

Garnish the finished cocktail with a single wedge of fresh lime. Place the wedge of lime on the rim of the glass. This cocktail can be served with half the egg whites of a regular-sized egg. (The egg is optional and is entirely up to you.)

Ingredients:

- 66 ml of white rum (light variant)
- 22 ml of triple sec
- 33 ml of freshly squeezed lemon juice
- 33 ml of lime cordial

ANGOSTURA WHISKEY

Serve the Angostura Whiskey cocktail in a rock glass. Shake all the ingredients, strain, and pour into the glass with three or four ice cubes. The garnish for this cocktail is a single citrus twist, preferably lemon.

Ingredients:

- 88 ml of bourbon whiskey
- 22 ml of Galiliano liqueur
- 11 ml of sugar syrup
- 2.7 ml of Angostura bitters flavoring

LIME & RUM TANGO

Serve this violet-hued cocktail in a tall Collin's glass. Shake all ingredients, add crushed ice to the glass, and pour. (Don't forget to strain!) Finish the cocktail with a wedge of fresh lime on top of the floating crushed ice.

Ingredients:

- 88 ml of white rum (light variant)
- 22 ml of fresh lime juice
- 33 ml of Velvet Felernum liqueur
- 1.8 ml of Peychaud's bitters flavoring

VERMOUTH DOMINATION

Serve Vermouth Domination in a long-stemmed martini glass. No ice cubes needed for this cocktail! Simply shake, strain, and pour into a chilled martini glass. Add a citrus zest (lemon) inside the glass after pouring the cocktail.

Ingredients:

- 88 ml of Scotch whisky
- 44 ml of vermouth (sweet variant)
- 44 ml of vermouth (dry variant)
- 2.7 ml of Angostura bitters flavoring

ENERGIZING SHOT OF TEQUILA

Serve this cocktail in a short, heavy-bottomed shot glass. All ingredients must be chilled prior to the creation of the cocktail. The shot glass must also be chilled. Layer the ingredients in the order given below.

Ingredients:

- 33 ml of coffee liqueur
- 33 ml of tequila

MINTY CHOCOLATE VODKA

Serve the Chocolate Vodka in a single shot glass. Shake all ingredients, strain, and pour into a glass that has been previously chilled.

Ingredients:

- 22 ml of vodka
- 22 ml of white cream of chocolate
- 22 ml of green cream of mint

THE KNOCKBACK COCKTAIL

With a potent mix of four venerable alcoholic spirits, the Knockback Cocktail is a prime choice for the discerning drinker who knows how to imbibe. Serve the Knockback Cocktail in a chilled, long-stemmed martini glass. Shake all the ingredients in a Boston shaker, strain, and pour into the glass. Garnish the finished cocktail with a citrus twist (lemon).

Ingredients:

- 44 ml of white rum (light variant)
- 22 ml of vermouth (dry variant)
- 22 ml of cognac
- 22 ml of dry gin
- 11 ml of fresh lime juice
- 11 ml of sugar syrup
- 22 ml of water (alternatively, you can add wet ice to the cocktail instead of 22 ml of water)

MINTY COFFEE SHOT

Refrigerate all the ingredients and chill the heavy-bottomed shot glass before making this cocktail. All ingredients must be layered into the shot glass -- not shaken or stirred.

Ingredients:

- 22 ml of coffee liqueur
- 22 ml of white cream of mint
- 22 ml of cream liqueur

ORANGE BITTERS MIX

Serve the Orange Bitters Mix in a chilled, long-stemmed martini glass. Mix the ingredients in a tall mixing glass, stir for a few seconds, and pour into the martini glass. No ice cubes are needed for this cocktail recipe.

Ingredients:

- 88 ml of fino sherry
- 44 ml of vermouth (sweet variant)
- .18 ml of orange bitters flavoring

NECTAR OF THE GODS

Serve the Nectar of the Gods in a heavy-bottomed, long-stemmed martini glass. In a Boston shaker, pour the honey *first* and the rum second. Use a stirrer to dissolve the honey.

Add the rest of the ingredients, shake for twenty seconds, and strain. No ice cubes are needed. Different kinds of honey can be used for this recipe -- taste, taste, taste! Finish the cocktail with a wedge of fresh lime on top of the martini glass.

Ingredients:

- 88 ml of rum
- 3.75 ml of honey (thin, runny variant)
- 22 ml of fresh lime juice
- 22 ml of water

ORANGE-HONEY TANGO

Serve the Orange-Honey Tango in a long-stemmed martini glass. Chill the glass before serving this cocktail. Pour the honey into the Boston shaker first before adding the rum.

Mix with a stirrer to dissolve the honey. Add the ingredients and shake for twenty seconds. Strain and serve. Finish the cocktail with a fresh mint leaf on top of the cocktail, and a layer of champagne added *after* the initial mix has been poured into the martini glass.

Ingredients:

- 44 ml of rum (golden variant)
- 5 ml of honey (runny variant)
- 22 ml of fresh lime juice
- 22 ml of fresh orange juice
- 11 ml of champagne

BLOODY MARY WITH CAMPARI

Serve this cocktail in a tall cocktail glass like a Collin's glass. Chill the glass before pouring the cocktail. Shake all ingredients, strain, and serve. Finish the cocktail with a fresh wedge of lime on top of the Collin's glass.

Ingredients:

- 88 ml of Campari
- 44 ml of vodka
- 154 ml of fresh grapefruit juice

FRESH N' FRUITY BLOODY MARY

Serve the Fresh N' Fruity Bloody Mary in a tall cocktail glass. Use a muddler to crush the fresh raspberries. If you don't have a muddler, any clean pestle will do. This should be done in the Boston shaker, not on a plate or mixing glass. Add the remaining ingredients and shake. Add three or four ice cubes before pouring the cocktail. Finish the cocktail by adding fresh raspberries on top.

Ingredients:

- 8 pieces of raspberries (fresh fruit is a must)
- 88 ml of vodka with orange zest
- 22 ml of raspberry-flavored liqueur
- 66 ml of fresh orange juice
- 55 ml of cranberry juice (commercial juice can be used)
- 22 ml of fresh lime juice

QUICK N' FEISTY BLOODY MARY

For this cocktail, you'll need a tall, chilled cocktail glass like a Collin's glass. Simply shake the ingredients in a Boston shaker and finish with a single, pickled bean garnish.

Ingredients:

- 88 ml of vodka
- 176 ml of ciamato juice
- 22 ml of fresh lime juice
- .35 ml of classic Tabasco pepper sauce
- 2.7 ml of Worcestershire sauce
- 2 pinches of salt
- 2 pinches of ground pepper

Bowe Packer

BLOODY MARY WITH SAKE

Serve this Bloody Mary variant in a tall cocktail glass and finish the cocktail with a single stick of lemongrass. After shaking and pouring the cocktail, simply place the lemongrass stick into the cocktail before serving.

Ingredients:

- 132 ml of sake
- 132 ml of tomato juice (pressed juice)
- 22 ml of fresh lemon juice
- .4 ml of classic Tabasco pepper sauce
- 3.6 ml of Worcestershire sauce
- 2 pinches of salt
- 2 pinches of ground pepper

BLOODY MARY WITH TEQUILA

Serve the Bloody Mary with Tequila in a tall cocktail glass with a four ice cubes. Shake the ingredients, strain, and pour.

Finish the cocktail with two garnishes: the rim of the Collin's glass must be lined with ground pepper and salt, and the final cocktail must also have a celery stick. For the modern take on this beloved classic, simply add 88 ml of vodka to this mix.

Ingredients:

- 88 ml of tequila
- 176 ml of tomato juice (pressed)
- 22 ml of fresh lemon juice
- .4 ml of classic Tabasco pepper sauce
- 3.6 ml of Worcestershire sauce
- 1.25 ml of horseradish sauce
- 22 ml of Tawny port
- 2 pinches of salt
- 2 pinches of ground pepper

CREAMY ALEXANDER

Serve the Creamy Alexander in a heavy-bottomed, long-stemmed martini glass. Chill the glass before serving. Mix the ingredients in a Boston shaker, strain, and serve. No ice cubes are needed for this cocktail.

Ingredients:

- 66 ml of dry gin
- 44 ml of white cream of chocolate
- 33 ml of heavy cream
- 33 ml of fresh milk

ENERGIZING ALEXANDER

Serve the Energizing Alexander in a chilled, regular martini glass. Shake the ingredients, strain, and pour into the martini glass. No ice cubes are needed. Garnish the resulting cocktail with nutmeg. Grate the nutmeg on top of the finished cocktail -- lightly move the grate across the cocktail to evenly distribute the grated nutmeg.

Ingredients:

- 66 ml of vodka
- 22 ml of coffee liqueur
- 22 ml of white cream of chocolate
- 55 ml of heavy cream
- 55 ml of fresh milk

MINTY ALEXANDER

Serve the Minty Alexander in any available martini glass. Garnish the resulting cocktail with a single, fresh mint leaf. The glass should be chilled before the cocktail is strained and poured.

Ingredients:

- 66 ml of dry gin
- 55 ml of white cream of chocolate
- 55 ml of heavy cream
- 55 ml of milk

MELON COCONUT SENSATION

Serve the Melon Coconut Sensation in a tall Collin's glass. Chill the glass before pouring the finished cocktail. Before serving, garnish the Melon Coconut Sensation with a wedge of fresh lime.

Ingredients:

- 88 ml of vodka
- 22 ml of melon-flavored liqueur
- 22 ml of coconut rum liqueur
- 132 ml of fresh pineapple juice

RUM-TEQUILA EXPLOSION

Use a heavy-bottomed shot glass for this cocktail. Place the ingredients in the refrigerator before serving. The shot glass must also be chilled. Layer the ingredients in the order they're listed below.

Ingredients:

- 22 ml of coffee liqueur
- 22 ml of tequila
- 22 ml of rum (54.5% proof)

APRICOT PISCO MIX

Serve this cocktail in a long-stemmed martini glass. No ice cubes are needed for this cocktail. Chill the martini glass for a minute before straining and pouring the drink. Finish the cocktail by adding a citrus twist on the rim of the martini glass (orange is preferred).

Ingredients:

- 88 ml of Pisco
- 22 ml of triple sec
- 22 ml of apricot brandy
- 33 ml of water

Aromatic Whiskey Cocktail

Serve the Aromatic Whiskey Cocktail in a heavy-bottomed rock glass. Place the ingredients in a Boston shaker, shake for twenty seconds, and strain before pouring. Place three to four cubes of ice in the rock glass before pouring the Aromatic Whiskey Cocktail. Garnish the finished cocktail with a fresh stemmed cherry.

Ingredients:

- 88 ml of whiskey (rye variant)
- 55 ml of vermouth (dry variant)
- 55 ml of fresh pineapple juice
- 1.8 ml of Peychaud's bitters flavoring

APPLE ALMOND MIX

Serve the Apple Almond Mix in a chilled, long-stemmed martini glass. No ice cubes are necessary. Strain and pour the cocktail into the glass, and drop three roasted almond beans as garnishing.

Ingredients:

- 88 ml of vodka
- 22 ml of fresh lemon juice
- 22 ml of almond-flavored syrup
- 44 ml of fresh apple juice
- 1.8 ml of peach bitters flavoring

SWEET APPLE VODKA

Serve the Sweet Apple Vodka cocktail in a chilled Collin's glass. With a pestle or muddler, press the fresh ginger slices on the bottom of the Boston shaker. After muddling this ingredient, add the rest of the ingredients and proceed as usual. Strain the cocktail and pour into the Collin's glass. The Collin's glass must have crushed ice prior to the pouring. Finish the cocktail by grating nutmeg over it. Distribute the nutmeg dust evenly throughout the surface of the cocktail. Place a wedge of fresh apple on top of the glass.

Ingredients:

- 4 pieces of sliced, fresh ginger
- 66 ml of bison vodka
- 176 ml of fresh apple juice
- 22 ml of sugar syrup
- 22 ml of apple schnapps liqueur

COGNAC SURPRISE

Serve the Cognac Surprise in a regular flute champagne glass. Shake all the ingredients, strain, and pour into the glass. The flute glass may or may not be chilled. Top the finished cocktail with a small amount of champagne.

Ingredients:

- 44 ml of Remy Martin cognac
- 44 ml of Boulard Calvados (or any apple-flavored aperitif)
- 11 ml of fresh lemon juice
- 11 ml of triple sec
- 11 ml of champagne

FRUITY WHISKEY MIX

Serve the Fruity Whiskey Mix in a regular, long-stemmed martini glass. Chill the glass before pouring the finished cocktail. Garnish the Fruity Whisky Mix with a single, thin slice of apple on top. Shake the cocktail, strain, and serve.

Ingredients:

- 66 ml of bourbon whiskey
- 22 ml of apple schnapps liqueur
- 22 ml of crème de myrtille
- 33 ml of cranberry juice
- 22 ml of fresh apple juice
- 11 ml of fresh lime juice

A Rose By Any Name

For this cocktail, you'll need a large martini glass -- one that can hold at least ten fluid ounces. Shake all the ingredients, strain, and pour into the chilled glass. Pour the red wine last. Garnish the drink with a single rose petal. Lightly place the rose petal on the drink so that it floats.

Ingredients:

- 110 ml of Remy Martin cognac
- 22 ml of vermouth (dry variant)
- 22 ml of cream of mint pastille
- 22 ml of fresh orange juice
- 22 ml of grenadine syrup
- 33 ml of water
- 11 ml of red wine

SWEET WHISKEY MIX

Serve the Sweet Whiskey Mix in a flute champagne glass. Shake all the ingredients *except* the champagne and the bourbon. After shaking, straining, and pouring, pour the bourbon on top. Top the drink with champagne last. Garnish the cocktail with a slice of fresh peach. Coat the sugar cube with the Angostura bitters flavoring agent and drop the same into the finished cocktail.

Ingredients:

- 1 sugar cube
- 3.6 ml of Angostura bitters flavoring
- 22 ml of bourbon whiskey
- 22 ml of champagne

RIDING WITH CAMPARI

Serve this cocktail in a tall Collin's glass that has been chilled. Shake the cocktail ingredients, strain, and pour. Garnish the cocktail with a single slice of fresh orange. Place three to four cubes of ice before pouring.

Ingredients:

- 88 ml of Campari
- 88 ml of vermouth (sweet variant)
- 11 ml of soda water

CREAMY, MINTY VERMOUTH

Serve the Creamy, Minty Vermouth in a regular, long-stemmed martini glass. Shake the cocktail ingredients, strain, and pour. Pour the port last, and garnish the finished drink with a single fresh mint leaf.

Ingredients:

- 44 ml of Remy Martin cognac
- 44 ml of vermouth (dry variant)
- 11 ml of cream of mint
- 44 ml of fresh orange juice
- 22 ml of grenadine syrup
- 22 ml of Tawny port

A WORLD OF ORANGE

Serve this cocktail in a long-stemmed martini glass. No ice cubes are needed for this recipe. Chill the martini glass for a minute before pouring the strained cocktail. Garnish with a citrus twist (orange).

Ingredients:

- 88 ml of Bokma Genever
- 44 ml of triple sec
- 44 ml of fresh orange juice
- 2.7 ml of orange bitters flavoring

Anise Vodka Mix

Serve this cocktail in a regular martini glass. With a regular pestle or muddler, crush the star anise in the Boston shaker. Proceed to add the other ingredients. Shake and strain. Pour into the chilled martini glass and top the finished cocktail with a whole star anise (dried).

Ingredients:

- 2 pieces of star anise (dried)
- 44 ml of vodka
- 33 ml of Luxardo Cesari
- 22 ml of anise liquor
- 66 ml of water

POWER WITH CHERRY ON TOP

For this drink, you'll need a tall sling glass that has been previously chilled. Shake all the ingredients of the cocktail *except* the champagne. When the cocktail has been shaken and poured, add the champagne and stir the cocktail for a few seconds. Top the finished drink with a slice of fresh lemon and a stemmed cherry. The sling glass should have four to give ice cubes.

Ingredients:

- 22 ml of triple sec
- 22 ml of tequila
- 22 ml of white rum (light variant)
- 22 ml of dry gin
- 22 ml of vodka
- 22 ml of fresh lime juice
- 22 ml of sugar syrup
- 11 ml of champagne

CREAMY MELON SHOT

You'll need a heavy-bottomed shot glass for this recipe. Chill the ingredients and the glass before making the cocktail. Layer the ingredients in the order they're listed below.

Ingredients:

- 33 ml of coffee liqueur
- 22 ml of melon-flavored liqueur
- 22 ml of cream liqueur

Vanilla Apple Sophistication

Serve the Vanilla Apple Sophistication in a heavy-bottom, long-stemmed martini glass. Shake the cocktail ingredients, strain, and pour into a chilled glass. Garnish the finished cocktail with a single slice of fresh apple on the rim of the martini glass.

Ingredients:

- 88 ml of advocaat liqueur
- 66 ml of Boulard Calvados
- 22 ml of apple schnapps liqueur
- 11 ml of vanilla syrup

ELDERFLOWER MIST

Serve the Elderflower Mist cocktail in a tall cocktail glass, like a Collin's glass. Place three to four ice cubes in the Collin's glass before pouring the shaken cocktail. Put a straw in the drink. Garnish the finished cocktail with a slice of fresh lemon.

Ingredients:

- 66 ml of dry gin
- 44 ml of elderflower liqueur
- 44 ml of apple schnapps liqueur
- 44 ml of fresh lime juice
- 11 ml of soda water

BLACKBERRY SOOTHER

Crush the fresh blackberries in the Boston shaker with the help of a pestle or muddler. Add the rest of the ingredients *except* the heavy cream. Shake and strain.

Pour the resulting mix into a chilled martini glass. Place the heavy cream on top of the creation with the help of a spoon. Garnish the finished cocktail by grating fresh nutmeg on top and adding a single, fresh blackberry on the rim of the martini glass.

Ingredients:

- 7 fresh blackberries
- 88 ml of vodka
- 44 ml of fresh apple juice
- 22 ml of heavy cream

Vodka 3 Cocktail

This is a very simple and straightforward cocktail that should be served in a long-stemmed martini glass. Chill the glass first before pouring the shaken cocktail. Garnish the finished cocktail with a very thin slice of fresh apple. The slice should be thin enough to float on the surface of the finished drink.

Ingredients:

- 77 ml of vodka
- 44 ml of elderflower liqueur
- 55 ml fresh apple juice

TEQUILA & LIME MIX

Serve the Tequila & Lime Mix in a large martini glass -- one that can hold at least ten fluid ounces. Shake the ingredients and strain. Place about twelve ounces of crushed ice or shaved ice in the martini glass before pouring the cocktail. Garnish the cocktail with a lime wedge.

Ingredients:

- 88 ml of tequila
- 44 ml of fresh lime juice
- 22 ml of grenadine syrup
- 88 ml of orange flower water

APRICOT & APPLE WHISKEY TANGO

Serve this cocktail in a rock glass filled with three to four cubes of ice. Spoon the apricot jam into the Boston shaker and pour the bourbon. Dissolve the jam before mixing the other ingredients. Garnish the cocktail with a citrus twist (preferably lemon).

Ingredients:

- 5 ml of apricot jam
- 66 ml of bourbon whiskey
- 22 ml of apricot brandy
- 44 ml of fresh apple juice
- 22 ml of fresh lemon juice

CHERRY CLASSIC

Serve the Cherry Classic cocktail in a heavy-bottomed rock glass. Shake and strain the finished cocktail into a pre-chilled glass. You can place a stemmed cherry on top of the cocktail if you wish. Place ice cubes in the rock glass before pouring the cocktail.

Ingredients:

- 88 ml of Scotch whiskey
- 44 ml of cherry liqueur (this is actually a brandy)
- 66 ml of cranberry juice

ALMOND & LEMON SOOTHER

Serve this cocktail in a long-stemmed martini glass that has been previously chilled. Shake the ingredients for twenty seconds, strain carefully, and pour into the glass. Garnish with a citrus twist (lemon).

Ingredients:

- 88 ml of dry gin
- 22 ml of fresh lemon juice
- 11 ml of almond-flavored syrup
- 22 ml of water

ORIENTAL BLOODY MARY VARIANT

This tasty cocktail should be served in a tall cocktail glass (Collin's glass) that has been chilled. With a pestle or muddler, crush the ginger in the Boston shaker, and then add a measure of vodka.

Use a mixing spoon to add the wasabi to the existing mix. After the wasabi has been integrated, add the rest of the cocktail's ingredients. Shake for twenty seconds and strain. Pour over ice. Add lemongrass to the final concoction.

Ingredients:

- 3 pieces of sliced ginger
- 2.5 ml of Japanese wasabi paste
- 88 ml of Citroen vodka
- 2.5 ml of soy sauce
- 176 ml of tomato sauce
- 22 ml of lemon juice

LEMON MOCKTAIL

Serve the Lemon Mocktail in a tall Collin's glass. Shake the ingredients, strain, and pour over ice. Add a single slice of fresh lemon before serving.

Ingredients:

- 88 ml of fresh lemon juice
- 44 ml of sugar syrup
- 132 ml of cold breakfast tea

LIGHT AND SWEET COCKTAIL

Serve the Light and Sweet Cocktail in a tall Collin's glass. Shake and strain the cocktail, and pour over ice cubes. Garnish the finished cocktail with a single slice of fresh orange.

Ingredients:

- 66 ml of light rum (white variant)
- 22 ml of apricot brandy
- 11 ml of Galliano liqueur
- 110 ml of fresh pineapple juice
- 22 ml of fresh lemon juice

Dangerous & Flavorful

This strong yet flavorful cocktail should be served in a long-stemmed martini glass. Shake all the ingredients except for the champagne. Pour into a chilled martini glass before layering the top with the champagne.

Ingredients:

- 66 ml of vodka
- 55 ml of cognac
- 22 ml of Amontillado sherry
- 11 ml of champagne

SWEET & CREAMY SHOT

Serve this cocktail in a chilled shot glass. All ingredients must be chilled prior to serving. Layer the ingredients carefully in the order they appear below:

Ingredients:

- 22 ml of coffee liqueur
- 22 ml of white cream of chocolate
- 22 ml of Southern Comfort liqueur

Rum & Coconut Mix

Serve the Rum & Coconut mix in a tall Collin's glass. Shake the ingredients and pour into tall cocktail glass with twelve ounces of crushed or shaved ice. Garnish the finished cocktail with a sprig of fresh mint, a single slice of pineapple and a stemmed cherry.

Ingredients:

- 110 ml of white rum (light variant)
- 132 ml of fresh pineapple juice
- 22 ml of cream of coconut

ABOUT THE AUTHOR

Hello, my name is Bowe Chaim Packer and I like to see myself as an open, *"wear my heart out on my sleeve"* kind of guy.

Some of the most important things to me in my life are:

- Laughing
- Kissing
- Holding hands
- Being playful
- Smiling
- Talking deeply with others
- Being loved
- Loving others
- Changing the world one person at a time (if my presence in your life doesn't make a difference then why am I here?) Hmmmmm, maybe that is a topic for another book. ;-)
- Learning from others (although often times I first resist). However, don't give up on me….
- Sharing ideas (no matter what they might be)
- Learning about others via most forms of contact.
- Traveling – hello, of course – almost forgot one of my favorite pass times.

Bowe Packer

Remember, LIFE is a journey for each and every one of us. We must never forget the things that are important to us or lose sight of what makes us happy.

28948056R00065

Printed in Poland
by Amazon Fulfillment
Poland Sp. z o.o., Wrocław